Data Analytics

Using Big Data Analytics For Business To Increase Profits And Create Happy Customers

D1571082

Matthew Adams

the trademark owner. All trademarks and brands within this book are for clarifying purposes only and are the owned by the owners themselves, not affiliated with this document.

Contents

Introduction

I want to thank you and congratulate you for purchasing Data Analytics: Using Big Data Analytics For Business To Increase Profits And Create Happy Customers.

This book contains proven steps and strategies on how to use everyday data to increase the profitability and customer satisfaction of your business. Analytics has risen to prominence in the last half century, and big businesses have been using it to solve optimization problems and increase productivity. They have seen increased customer satisfaction and a reduction in wasted resources. Data analytics and analysis is not just for large businesses though —businesses of all sizes can use already gathered information to increase revenue by analyzing easy to assemble data in a logical way that optimizes business strategy.

Data analysis is now in the hands of thousands of more businesses, but many businesses do not use analytics to increase their productivity. There is a strong belief that analytics is a complicated process that requires expensive outside consultants and difficult to learn software. The reality couldn't be further from this sentiment; the time is ripe for businesses of all sizes to use data in smart ways to improve their revenue and increase customer happiness. The democratization of analytic tools makes today the greatest time to learn how to use existing information to improve your business.

The goal of this book is to walk you through how modern analysis tools can benefit your business, simply, easily, and with minimal cost; . By the time you have completed this book, you will feel confident in understanding how to utilize popular analytic analytics tools to maximize your businesses business ' success. You will understand not only how to conduct such analysis, but will also have an easy to understand explanation for how statistical tools and models can benefit you, in real terms that benefits benefit your bottom line.

The time is now to get a leg up on your competition, to increase revenue through minimal business investment, and to understand exactly how your business functions and why you get repeat business from customers. You don't have to be a large business to benefit from analytics – you just have to have the drive and willpower to complete this book and expand your understanding of the hidden power of using information in the way that is most profitable to your business and pleases your customer base.

Thanks again for purchasing this book, I hope you enjoy it!

Chapter 1

An Introduction To Analytics

Our World And Data

Your business is enveloped in hidden data, data that can be used to increase productivity, revenue and customer satisfaction. The successful utilization of this data depends on the analysis of seemingly independent pieces of information to come up with a coherent theory for the success of your business and happiness of your customer base. In its most basic form, analytics is just this – organizing and processing data to benefit the user in various ways, typically for the purpose of optimization.

Analytics can be thought of as putting a microscope to individual aspects of your business, and using this newfound insight to solve problems that were previously hidden to the naked eye. Analytics acts as a microscope by taking disparate pieces of information and coupling them together to form a picture. We refer to these small pieces of information collectively as 'data'. Your business or enterprise already uses a basic form of analytics for its day-to-day operations. For example, the money that you use for reinvestment in your business is a known quantity, based on the expenses of rent, wages and product costs. Using these known pieces of information like your expending wages and rent, leaves you with a number for profits. While this is an incredibly simplistic look, and the pieces of data are somewhat related to each other, you are able to draw a conclusion on how much money is available for reinvestment in your business based on a calculation. If we imagine all analytics as various calculations derived from existing measurements, we can gleam all sorts of conclusions that will improve business operations.

Determining the amount of money that could be used for business expansion and reinvestment would be impossible to know without the data of rent, wages and product cost. It's quite logical that to solve the problem of how much money is left for reinvestment we take out the money that is used to keep the business running as it is. Now picture trying to solve another problem; a more complicated problem that does not have clear pieces of information that you can refer to. For example, if you own a gas station and are trying to determine how late your store should stay open, you may collect data referring to the number of customers that purchase gas every year and the operating costs of the store per hour. Using this information, you will certainly get a workable answer, but is it truly the best answer, and the one that maximizes profits? Probably not, as there is a myriad of more complicated factors. Your gas station must have stable hours throughout the year so that customers always know if you are available, so an useable answer must be workable for every single day the business is operating. You must consider the time frame that you are looking at for determining optimal store hours – using a sample of purchases made throughout a week gives you a very incomplete answer. It would not account for seasonal changes, or account for the week's sample not being a normal purchasing week. You would have to incorporate data about the operating costs per season, looking for trends that indicate higher or lower numbers of customers during the winter or summer months. Using this data on a larger time scale, we can more effectively determine the optimal operating hours of the gas station. You may also want to change the metric by which you measure if your store should stay open. What's more important, foot traffic or actual purchases made. Even a simple question like store hours can lead to many different assumptions about what data is useful in determining the answer. Established statistical models provide our best bet in ruling out unhelpful factors, providing the best operating hours and most importantly, curtailing the 'sometimes less than helpful' solutions thought of through natural human intuition. One of the more famous examples of using statistics to come up with a better solution than human intuition comes from baseball.

Michael Lewis may have single-handedly changed the game of baseball when he used statistical analysis to determine the best draft picks for the Oakland Athletics Major League Baseball team. While his model is well accepted today as being something of a stroke of genius, it certainly wasn't accepted as the best practice at first. Draft picks should be based on player scouts, managers, coaches and team owners. The best choice to make in a draft is far more complicated than human intuition can compute. In fact, the best choices are often counter-intuitive, and can only be revealed through statistical models.

This is only one type of analytic. Both the problem of the gas station and picking optimal draft picks are based on solving an established question. There are other forms of analytics where problems that we did not ask ourselves can be made in the same way that statistical models reveal the best draft picks. By effectively collecting data and using the right analyzation tools, we can solve problems that we didn't even know existed. Suppose, for example, you are managing a supermarket and decide that you will keep extensive records of a few data points: products and the quantity purchased, profit margins on products and shelf placement of products. There is no initial question posed that would utilize this data; however, by using a basic statistical model that correlates (finds connections between) data points, you may find that where a product is placed on a shelf does not relate to how frequently that product is purchased. This would allow you to take items that are purchased at a similar rate, regardless of placement, and move them to lower shelves to make room for less popular items. The idea here is that by increasing the visibility on less popular items, you could encourage sales, all the while knowing that you are not hindering the sales of the popular products that you moved down several shelves closer to the floor. This analysis has created an optimization that you were not previously striving for. Notice also that the data collected in this supermarket were in three parts: sales, profit margins and product placement, and yet profit margins were not incorporated in this optimization. This is a key aspect to this side of analytics; some data will be useful and others will not, but without using statistics, it is impossible to rule out the important factors.

Both of the above examples involving the gas station and the supermarket are simplistic approaches to analytics, and these hypothetical examples are simply to illustrate the usefulness of analytics and how they relate to business. Before diving into how to use cases for specific types of analytics, there are some standard archetypes of analyses that all businesses can use to increase profitability, or solve other optimization problems. Each method of analysis requires further calculation to solve complex problems, but in their most basic form, there are three types of analytics:

Exploratory Data Analysis – Collecting data and determining the best way to process that data requires that we understand the data collected. Exploratory data analysis allows users to sort through troves of data to determine its usefulness. There are key metrics that we can use to understand the data more clearly. For example, let's say you took the height and weight of two hundred random people from all over the United States; looking at any individual number is not of any help, however by running very simple calculations, like the average, we can understand this data far more clearly. Whereas, it is impossible to simply communicate using two hundred data points; an average will tell us the basic height and weight of an American. How data will be used is best determined through this form of exploratory analysis. With our weight and height example, a business decision could be made about how many passengers can safely ride in a plane by using the average weight of a passenger. When the measurements were taken, it wasn't known that this would be the final use, but now that the data is collected, the average allows us to realize the data's utility. Another example would be if we took the mode, or number that occurs most frequently in a data set. A clothing company could use this number to produce t-shirts in quantities that would accurately represent the population they are trying to sell to. These are two very basic calculations that could be run on the datasets, but there is a lot of other useful information hidden in the data as well. Running calculations and understanding what they mean can determine how the data will be used when no clear goal is in mind.

Confirmatory Data Analysis – When a clear goal is in mind, confirmatory data analysis can be used to either confirm or deny a hypothesis. This has applications for businesses and the sciences, and is the forefront type of analysis that is taught throughout schools in America. A business will use this type of analysis to test a hypothesis in pretty much the same way a scientist would. For example, suppose a business wanted to know if increasing the data allotment on a cell phone plan increases the number of app purchases made by a user. This is an important problem to solve if the service provider receives a portion of all application sales from either the Google or Apple app stores. This would encourage a cell provider to lower the cost of data plans to maximize profits through driving sales in app stores. We are just at the tip of the iceberg for data analytics, so more complicated questions like 'What is the optimal price of data plans to maximize revenue from app purchases?' are not our current focus. We are instead looking at whether or not that question is even worth asking – to do this, we must find the relationship between data plans and app purchases. Sticking to simple statistical methods for this section, a regression analysis would provide an answer to our question.

It's possible that you've heard of regression analysis but even if you haven't, the basic principle is quite simple – using two or more data sets, a number between zero and one will indicate if the data sets are correlated. That is, a correlation of *one* would mean 100% correlation, or in our example, every customer that has more data, will always make more app purchases. A correlation of *zero* would indicate that there is a 0% correlation between data and app purchases. No matter how much data you give a customer, they will always make the same number of app purchases regardless.

Notice that the regression gives a percentage correlation between zero and one, and that this represents between 0% and 100% correlation. It's important to note that this correlation does not indicate the *magnitude* for data or app purchases. This means that our regression does not tell us *how much more data* a customer needs to increase his or her app purchases. The cell provider might have to give a customer eight additional gigabytes of data to have them spend one more dollar in the app store, or it could be five hundred megabytes more data, meaning one hundred dollars more spent in the app store. To summarize, a regression only tell us *if* there is a relationship between two or more data sets, and nothing more. In our example of data plans and app purchases, we have solved a single problem. We know the relationship between data and app purchases. Other calculations are necessary to solve the ideal price of data plans to maximize app purchases. The important thing of note about confirmatory data analysis is that we start with a question or theory, and then move to testing this theory.

- **Qualitative Data Analysis** – Best explained as the *why;* qualitative data answers the question of why the data comes out the way it does. Let's go back to our example of data plans and app purchases from the last section for a moment. Through confirmatory data analysis, we know if there is a relationship between increased data and more app purchases. Let us suppose that our regression from this example showed a 100% correlation. That is, increasing data always led to more app purchases. To answer the question of why this is true, we need a different type of data set than in our previous two forms of analysis. To best answer this question, a qualitative survey given to customers would provide the most accurate answer for why customers make more app purchases. The best qualitative data that businesses collect comes from survey data like this, where customers are given direct questions and their answers recorded. Note that unlike other forms of analyses, qualitative data does not always present itself as numbers. Most large scale surveys pose questions that allow for numeric responses such as, 'From one to ten, how much did you enjoy our product?' However, the question we posed with data plans is far more nuanced. Our best answer comes in the form of written survey data. This data is more much difficult to sort through, but our question is asked directly and our answer is plain to see. A huge drawback of this survey is the limited population of whom we could collect responses from. It would be unreasonable to collect more than a few hundred responses from customers, and within this pile, there will be useless data such as incomplete surveys, fake responses and entirely blank forms. There is another way to conduct qualitative analysis, one that would allow for a much larger sample size of customers – the challenge is in how the service provider would create a larger scale survey.

The only way to get data from thousands of respondents is by collecting answers that are represented through numerical data points. If we are still focusing on *why* customers buy more apps when given more data, the creators of the survey would have to come up with savvy questions that determine our answer through numeric responses. For example, a few questions that will allow for a similarly qualitative response as our written survey data: "During what times of the day do you make purchases from the app store?" – Here, the answers would be organized as 1PM-2PM, 3PM-4PM, etc. "Do you make more purchases in the app store at home or when out of the house?" – The answers here are organized as a binary choice between at home or out of the home. "Would you say you make a majority of app purchases on a Wi-Fi network or the cellular network?" – The answers here would be Wi-Fi, cell network, or "I don't know."

Let's review what the creator of our survey is trying to accomplish in all three questions. With the first question, the survey creator can relate the hours that customers frequently make purchases, with when they are likely not home. The survey creator would know that most people work outside of the home during the day, a statistic attainable through historical data. This would have the customer answer whether they do most of their shopping from home or at work, importantly, without the customer knowing what question the survey is trying to answer. The second question is straight forward, but the significance is greater than the question first appears; it actually tells the cell company where customers *enjoy* making their purchases, again without the customer knowing that this is what the survey is after. Lastly, the third question asks customers on what network they make most of their purchases. The answers match the question directly, but importantly, there is a third option for customers that are not sure of what network they are on when they make purchases. This third option makes the survey data much more useful, as without it, a number of customers will answer the question incorrectly because they simply do not know, but are not presented with an option to abstain from the question. Our survey creator now knows the answer to all three of these questions, but for a significantly larger population than if they had conducted a write-in survey.

In both methods of collecting survey data, the service provider has conducted qualitative data collection. The write-in survey data is clearly qualitative and cannot be represented in numeric form. In the second survey that poses three questions with multiple choice responses, our survey creator can organize the data much more clearly. Each of these methods has advantages and disadvantages, but both serve to answer the question of *why* customers make more purchases when they have increased data. The write-in survey asks the customer directly, and the responses answer our question clearly, but the sample size is small. The three question survey reaches far more people, but the creator of the survey is making an inference that their questions can be turned into an answer for the question of *why*. Both are qualitative but are conducted in very different ways.

Key Terms, Explained Simply

Time Series – The best way to predict future outcomes is through finding cycles in the past. Time series, and time series analysis, entail finding cycles that exist and use them to predict the future of the cycle. There are many examples of this in nature, politics and business.

In nature, sun spots are cyclic, as are tides and the phases of the moon. We know exactly what portion of the moon is going to be visible, or when tides will be high or low, because of past cycles. An example of nature that does not fall within cycles is the weekly weather forecast – this is not cyclic behavior, however the seasons and average temperatures that accompany them are cyclic.

In United States politics, there are clear cycles that can be used to predict presidencies, congressional seats and senate seats. These are not nearly as accurate as the natural cycles described above. An example of this is the rotational seat theory of presidential governance. This is the idea that one party, republican or democrat, can only hold the white house for one to two election cycles before it goes to the other party. At the time that this book is being written, Hillary Clinton seems likely to win the presidency for 2016. This would fall outside of the standard theory of white house rotation, but does not dismiss the entire theory. Use this as an example that cycles are guidelines, and that there are always examples that fall outside of a cycle. This does not damn the entire cycle as a whole, because there is enough evidence to support that this cycle is *generally* true.

In business, cycles can be found in the high and low points of sales for the year. For example, the fall season is commonly a point of the highest profits for companies that sell directly to consumers. Customer shopping is up during this period and so sales are greater than at other points of the year. Businesses use this known cycle to ramp up hiring in the fall months. Another example comes in the form of computers. Moore's law falls under a business cycle, and states that approximately every eighteen months, the number of transistors that can fit in a given space doubles. Again, there are times when the number is above or below this two times figure, however businesses still use this law to great effect. Software developers can anticipate the available consumer hardware so as to develop for the future. Computer resellers like Dell or Apple can plan revisions on their hardware according to this model as well.

Portfolio Analytics – Determining the interest rates on loans for a number of consumers, portfolio analytics finds the inherit risk in providing loans. This is not done on a per customer level, but rather on sets of customers. The best way to think about this is mortgage backed securities. Acknowledging that there was a tremendous failure in 2008, the principle behind these securities is actually quite solid. There is a tremendous number of contributing factors to the 2008 financial crisis, but one of the main factors was fraud, as in home owners that declared income incorrectly, or real estate agents that participated in predatory lending to individuals that could not afford the homes they were sold. The math behind these securities absolutely works, but these cases of fraud (along with many other factors) distorted the numbers to the point of near worldwide economic ruin.

A mortgage backed security works by bundling multiple mortgages together into a single package, or security. These securities have their overall risk calculated by using the risk for each individual mortgage in the security. A security could be perfectly safe to buy even if a number of people default on their mortgages, because there are enough low risk mortgages to balance out the entire security. I use this type of security to demonstrate portfolio analytics because it has been a frequent topic in the news for many years, and most people have at least heard of it, however there are other examples. Mutual funds operate in much the same way, being able to fairly and accurately predict the amount of return on investment by spreading risk across multiple stocks, bonds and commodities. The math behind a successful portfolio analysis is complex; however, the purpose is always the same: lower the overall risk of an investment portfolio by diversifying investments. How those investments are diversified is the action of the complex math behind the scenes of portfolio analytics.

ϑ **Risk Analytics** – Portfolio analytics is the calculation of risk for a bundle of investments, and requires risk analytics for the individual investments in that bundle. The math behind risk analytics is slightly less complex than on a portfolio; however the determining factors are more complex. In risk analytics, we are looking at an individual mortgage, stock or even person, and calculating risk based on a variety of factors. This risk is used to determine whether a loan should be given out, what percentage the loan should be priced at, or whether or not an individual asset is risky. An example of this is an individual's credit score. This number is a complex calculation incorporating an individual's mortgage, credit card, salary and other factors. The end result is a fairly simple number that tells the degree to which an individual is credit worthy.

Breaking away from financials, another form of risk analytics comes in health care. Health care costs for *the many* are determined in the risk of individuals. The risk of an individual getting sick is calculated on simple factors like weight, height, smoker or non-smoker, and so forth. How this risk is represented is hidden to the consumer, much unlike a credit score which can be easily retrieved. However insurance companies calculate risk for individuals using various health metrics and sometimes, even family history.

Digital Analytics – How online ads are automatically purchased through algorithms is an example of digital analytics. Digital analytics have many use cases that extend far beyond the internet, but over the last fiver years, the term has become muddled. It is most commonly used to refer to the statistics of websites, such as traffic and unique users. This is why the term has become quite synonymous with marketing and purchasing web ads. However, the term more generally refers to the use of analytics for various optimization problems where the data sets used are well defined in the digital space. Explained simply, Google and other search engines use digital analytics to determine the order of search results. We call this digital analytics, because the data they are using to make such optimizations for their search engines comes from digital data that is hard to fake. For example, Google knows that the data on searches for specific terms cannot be forged and is very reliable. They know this because the data sets are so huge (in the billions) that factors that try to distort search engine optimizations can never succeed. If you have ever seen a comment on Facebook or other social media, insisting that you repeat a phrase to raise it to the top of Google, it is a fool's errand. Simply, so much data will wash out any attempted distortion on the part of human actors. This is why Google and other search engines are so reliable in their search results.

Additionally, digital analytics is sometimes used to describe government agencies attempting to prevent terrorist attacks or other acts of violence. This is referred to as digital analytics because the information largely comes from digital devices, but also because this information is hard to fake. It is difficult to spoof the location of a cell phone at various times of the day, or what cell phone towers it was used to communicate with. Again, the basic principle of using data that is hard to fake is at the core of digital analytics.

Security Analytics – Very commonly used in the same breath as digital analytics; this refers to the collection and use of data to ensure security across networks. For example, intrusions into businesses or governments are determined through security analytics. The data points collected here are the different nodes (think streets and roads) used to connect within a computer network.

All terms included in this section relate to business, including security analytics. Aside from determining if information was stolen from a business, it is also used to ensure the security of devices and user information. For example, a message that commonly appears when creating a password indicating how secure the password is. This is a result of calculations done to determine how hard it would be to *guess* that password if a computer has several thousand attempts. In other words, the complexity of a password is not to discourage a human from guessing the password, it is to deter an algorithm that would guess each and every alpha numeric character to hard break the password. Another example comes in how user information is stored, such as whether or not user data is encrypted (an additional layer of security). Security analytics is becoming ever more important in our digital society. Even small businesses need to be aware of issues that could stem from using computers or storing user data. This is very important when customer data is being used for other analytics – customers that have their data stolen lose tremendous trust in the organization that had the security failure.

Metadata – A contender for word of the year in 2013, metadata is the data that describes large data sets. It is extremely useful in security, government and analysis of large data sets. You might be familiar with the term as Edward Snowden popularized it earlier this decade, but the uses are often far less nefarious than how it originally gained its popularity. Metadata is a great way for businesses to collect data on customers, while ensuring that the privacy of individuals is still respected. For example, a car manufacturer may collect survey data on what states their cars are most popular. This means that a large company like Honda can determine that its cars are more popular in California, then perhaps Texas. While this data is collected from individuals, there is no reason to keep the name of each individual in the record, as it is superfluous information that only serves to limit that customer's privacy. The metadata in this example is the description of x number of Honda cars that are in California, and y number of the same car that is in Texas. It describes the data, without being granular enough to examine the individual from which the data was recorded. In this example, the data is useful to determine where more car dealerships should be opened, or where more advertisements should be purchased. It is likely that in your analytics, metadata will play some role, if not a very significant role.

Software Analytics – This form of analytics largely only affects software companies, but can have implications for small businesses specializing in other products as well. Software analytics is the analysis of the use case of a particular product, with the term stemming from its usage in software development. For example, the features that get improved, carried over or discontinued in software like Microsoft Office or the Prezi Presentation software suite, comes from the analysis of how many customers use a particular feature, how it is being used, and how frequently it is being used. For a company like Microsoft and their Office suite, features are carried over from year to year based on their popularity. New features are implemented based on the popularity of how the software is frequently used. The newest versions of Office include a major online component; this stems from analytics showing that documents are increasingly shared between two or more customers. If the end result of every document is emailing it to a coworker, then Microsoft knows that they must implement features that make this easier. At the same time, a feature that no one uses can be phased out and development resources used elsewhere.

In relation to small businesses that do not sell software, this form of analytics still has its uses. The data sets used to calculate what features need to be worked on or improved are very different, but the algorithms to determine customer satisfaction and use cases can be exactly the same. Any physical retail store can use these algorithms to calculate foot traffic within sections of a store. Best Buy, for example, can use software analytics to see where more team members are needed throughout the store. The key difference is where the data sets are coming from. For a software company, the data comes from the amount of time and number of customers that use a particular software feature. In a store like

Best Buy, it is the number of customers that visit a section of the store and how much time they spend in that section. You can see that while the data sets are different, they are both representing similar information – the frequency and number of customers that use a part of a business' product.

Chapter 2

The Importance Of Data Analysis In Business

Why Businesses Should Use Data Analytics – A Case Study

A business of any size can use data analytics to increase profits, customer satisfaction or automate tasks. In essence, data analytics is simply a tool for business owners and employees. Data can be used to automate small decisions or inform larger ones. Regardless of the size of the business, firms now have more data at their fingertips than ever before. Even if your business has few electronic records, there are more instances of digital information than you may realize. From credit payments to product orders, nearly all maintenance of a business includes useful information that can be used to great effect on a variety of cases. Let's take a look at a small firm and how they can utilize analytics to increase profits, reduce operating costs and increase customer satisfaction. Each problem posed can be solved using large data sets and the calculations necessary range from simple to medium in their complexity.

An independent coffee store has been operating in Kansas for ten years. It is a family owned business that is successful, but their reach has not extended beyond a single store. The owners make a decent wage, and have even saved enough money to open a second location. A question arises of where they should open up a second storefront, and to inform their decision, they decide to use analytics. Using free information available from their city, they can find the busiest roads in their local area. The data is available from their local government; they simply need to know what data corresponds to heavy traffic. Of available city records, they can find which roads have been repaved with the most frequency. This correlates to the most commonly used roads in their region. Using this data set, this family business can make a more informed decision. This is analytics in its simplest form. The data was collected by an outside agent, the data collection was free and the analysis done was as simple as looking through the history of road maintenance – no complex software or calculations necessary.

Our independent coffee store now has two locations, and they pose another question that large data sets can solve; at what times of the day should they brew fresh coffee? The owners know that customers love fresh coffee, and that they wouldn't serve a customer coffee that has been brewed and left to sit for too long. This comes with a problem; the overhead of throwing out old coffee can be reduced if they could just figure out the ideal times of the day in which to brew fresh coffee. Sure, there would be exceptions, but there is a general pattern to the number of customers that they have coming in and out of the store throughout the day. To solve for this problem, our small business needs two things. One, they need the data of the sales of coffee they make, preferably over a period of three or more months, and two, they need software to figure out the ideal times to brew coffee. The answer to their first step has likely already been recorded; they have the ledger for the sales that they've made the past few months. The second part of the question is easy; they will use SAS brand software for small businesses (more on this in chapter four). This is only one of many software solutions, but it's the one our small business owners choose. Using the software, they input *only* coffee sales and the times in which those sales are made. The longer the time period of the data they enter, the better. They use three months of data because it is a large enough data set, and it is a reasonable amount of data to enter into the software. They use a simple optimization tool to calculate when they should be brewing fresh coffee throughout the day. The gains that they make in reduced overhead costs might not be apparent right away, but looking at their finances over a month or two, they will see reduced operating costs.

The third problem our small coffee shop is going to tackle is in the range of products they offer to customers. They feel that introducing more products will not only increase sales, but will also increase customer satisfaction. To solve this problem of what new product to introduce, they will be using a customer survey they make themselves, and very simple software, Microsoft Excel. The customer survey is handed out to consumers at the time of purchase, with a list of products and instructions to circle the one(s) that appeal to customers the most. This includes a dark hot chocolate, a pumpkin spice latte and espresso. To incentivize the return of this survey, a free cup of coffee is offered when a customer returns the filled out form. Once they have their data, our small business makes a simple chart with the three products and the frequency in which customers indicated they would be interested in each. Using Excel, or even by hand if the survey respondents were limited, they calculate the basic statistic of the mode of their data set, or the most common answer. The pumpkin spice latte is by far the fan favorite, and so they expand their product line to include this new latte.

In this long form example, we see how a very small business can use data recovered, already collected or data gathered, to make informed decisions about how to run their business. The larger the firm, the greater the economies of scale, and the more returns can be gained from big data; however, all businesses can use analytics to drive sales and customer satisfaction; with today's tools and available information, it is easier than ever.

How Businesses Use Big Data

The basic types of analytical methods in chapter one lead us to how businesses adopt their methodology in determining more complex methods of advertising and decision making. The following are more specific analytical methods derived from the simple base of exploratory, confirmatory and qualitative data analytics:

Decision Analytics – Similar to our problem with optimizing for store hours for a gas station in chapter one, this form of analytics comprises of using known data to make the most informed decision. To get started, the user needs to know exactly what they wish to accomplish, or in many cases, what they would like to prioritize. In our gas station example, the goal was to determine what the optimal store hours are; however, just as important is how priorities should *inform* this decision. For example, while profits were used for solving the optimization problem, other considerations such as employee hours and safety concerns for operating a gas station late at night were not included in the optimization. A well thought out decision requires knowing precisely what one wants to accomplish, but will not typically aid in brining attention to new issues or problems outside of the optimization. Considering employee hours or safety would be up to the store owner, and the profit optimization would fail to consider these factors. It is also worth noting that as powerful as data analytics can be, potential long term consequences of potentially disgruntled employees, or having to eventually pay a larger salary due to safety concerns, are left entirely out of the equation. To include these factors is certainly possible, but the data required needs to be on a large enough time scale and include enough employees to be solved with any sort of accuracy.

A firm that would typically use this type of decision-making is an oil company. They must factor in increased wage hikes due to safety, and potentially more increased wage hikes due to difficulty in finding employees. The high salary that oil rig workers get paid, and their work schedule that frequently means working twelve to fourteen hour days for three weeks, followed by a full two weeks off, is the result of a complex decision made on the data from decades of oil workers before them. The tolerance for wage and hours was determined using an algorithm that accounted for these factors, and the answer was possible due to the extensive data the oil company has on its workers.

Descriptive Analytics – Most useful for sales and marketing, descriptive analytics organize data in a way that is simple to understand and digest. A great leader in this form of analysis is Amazon. Amazon has amassed a large amount of data on its customers. They have information about the products they purchase, the frequency of purchases, the bank these use, preference for form of payment (credit, cash, debit), and much more. Having a large amount of data is useless if it cannot be sorted and organized. Descriptive analytics does just this by categorizing customers based on some of the sample data above. Decision makers then look at these large categories and determine the best way to sell customers additional products.

For Amazon, this is done in two parts. One, the most common and the one you're probably familiar with, is the use of recommended products based on purchases. When a customer orders a product, Amazon recommends additional products based on customers that have purchased that same item. Sometimes this is indeed useful; however, many times it proves to be laughable. The algorithm is not *thinking* about the products that it recommends, and so it cannot see that there is little relation between a DVD and a type of hand soap. A recommendation for one product based on the other is made simply because some customers have made those purchases together. This is the equivalent of throwing out a large net in hope of some capture, no matter how small that capture is. The second way, and the one that is truly impressive, is the use of past purchasing data to categorize a customer as a whole. This manifests in the individualized customer home page that Amazon creates for each and every customer. The more the purchases over time, the more accurate this home page becomes as a representation of this person's individual preferences. Here, the use of big data is fully utilized; instead of relying on a small sample size of customers that purchased products together, Amazon uses their entire customer base to create a few hundred customer profiles. The information used to create a personalized profile is their entire customer base, and by increasingly attracting more customers, their categorization becomes more accurate. Also, as Amazon has increased in the range of products that they sell, so have their number of categorizations. A customer's home page will feature large categories of general interest to that customer, be it electronics, baby supplies and toys, or books of several dozen categories to themselves. This second method of descriptive analytics may seem like it should fall under decision analytics; however, the key difference here is that the decision and inferences made are done by human beings that created the categories for which customers fall into. If the computer algorithm produced the categories itself, this would fall more in line with decision analytics, with the original question posed relating to 'How to categorize our customer base?', and then allowing an algorithm to optimize for this question.

Predictive Analytics – Using past data to predict future outcomes, predictive analytics is an amalgamation of decision and descriptive analytics. Technically, Amazon's algorithm for recommending purchases based on customers that also purchased the same item would fall under this category, as well as descriptive analysis. Amazon's recommendation was if a customer has a product in their basket, this would be the simplest form of predictive analytics. They are using a very limited set of data points, typically only a few dozen, to determine what products a customer would also like to buy. This is why some of the recommendations in your basket can seem so out of place. To see one of the best uses of predictive analytics, we have to turn to the stock market and the rise of high frequency trading.

Most trades on the stock market are not done by humans

anymore. Instead, large volumes of trades are done by computers operating on complex algorithms predicting extremely short rises and falls in the values of various stocks. These algorithms incorporate a staggering amount of existing data on the stock market to make lighting fast decisions without any human intervention. This type of analytic has limited utility in customer facing businesses, as the best marketing to drive sales is still done by humans; nonetheless, in recent years, advertisements on the internet are increasingly purchased based on the predictive analytics of computers.

Five or ten years ago, if a company wanted to purchase banner ads for a new product, they would have to research websites that their customers frequent. Purchasing ads blindingly on an assortment of websites would be a large waste of capital, as the cost for throwing out such a large net is not equal to the number of customers it would attract. Marketers would use descriptive analytics to categorize different websites, and infer which websites would appeal to their customer base. Today, many of these ad purchases are done based on the data obtained from these earlier, human decided ad purchases. Companies have enough data to know the *general type* of website that attracts their customer; furthermore, a computer automatically purchases ad space on these websites. This illustrates, not only the usefulness of predictive analytics, but also the key difference between predictive and descriptive analysis, human decision-making versus computer decision-making.

Prescriptive Analytics – Taking predictive analytics one step further, prescriptive analytics not only predicts future behavior, but gives reasons for why that behavior may occur. In action, it is a harmony of computer decision-making and human input. Target uses this type of analytics to great effect, customizing the mailed advertisement that customers are sent. Computers determine the likelihood of products that will be purchased in the future based on existing data on that customer, as well as markers for how it came to this decision. Marketers then use this information to sell additional products based on the reasons *why* the algorithm predicted a customer's future outcome.

If this form of analytics sounds more confusing than the others, that's OK; it is an advanced type of analysis, but it can be easily understood using an example. Let's take a fictional family that has been shopping at target for many years, the Smiths. They purchase their groceries, cosmetics and utility items (garbage bags, etc.) from Target. This data, along with families that also purchase most of their products from Target, provides enough information to predict the need for future products. Based on the Smiths' purchases, an algorithm may start recommending baby formula, a stroller and diapers. The algorithm would also indicate the markers that led it to this prediction, which in this case, is a complicated formula incorporating every aspect of the Smiths' purchasing history. A marketer would look at this information and determine that someone in the Smith family is pregnant. This allows the marketer to customize mailed advertisements to a family that is expecting a baby. The computer contributes the products that should fill the flyer, and the marketer customizes the overall message of the flyer, for example, a banner with pictures of newborns. There are two important notes in this example, one, this type of predictive analysis can only be done with computer and human contributions. Two, the data required to accurately predict the Smiths' pregnancy is immense, including food, utility and other purchasing information. As a final note, if this type of marketing leaves a sour taste in your mouth, you are not alone. Target used to produce these types of flyers, indicating a pregnancy in the family, but has veered away from this type of advertising, as customers were rightly worried about the amount of data Target was collecting, and how it was processing this data.

Enterprise Decision Management – Relatively new in analytic approaches, enterprise decision management combines all of the above disciplines to make informed decisions on various problems and marketing strategies. As we progress, you can see that the types of analyses get more and more complicated. In describing prescriptive analytics, our example had a major corporation predicting whether or not a family was having a baby. Many see this as a step too far for companies and what they do with our data. The bottom line is that when customers are informed of the wide range of marketing techniques that involve big data, it can lead to a decline in sales. The sales technique a company wants to incorporate uses advanced algorithms to synthesize data, but if it only causes them to lose customers due to dissatisfaction in how their information in collected and processed, it is a poor strategy. Enterprise decision-making is the 'check' on the advanced algorithms and cutting edge marketing techniques that businesses use. It uses every discipline described so far to conclude how data should be used and what types of marketing strategies should be used. You can think of it as the rational human element in determining how computers and data should be used and collected, and that these decisions are made through simple experimentation.

Every business that uses big data must have a person or department dedicated to this type of decision-making. For example, in descriptive analytics, I discussed Amazon and their recommended products page, and how the recommendations range from useful to ridiculous. The decision to continue using the recommended products algorithm was determined based on testing whether or not it drives sales. A manager would disable the algorithm for some customers, and leave it running for others. To make sure that their two groups were of similar types of customers, they would use descriptive analytics to ensure the customers were in a similar category. In the example with the Smith family and Target, a manger would look at sales data and other metrics to determine if their use of predictive analytics was worth the hit to their overall reputation. The decision to use advanced algorithms are often determined with aid of algorithms that are just complex – the key is that managers are testing different hypotheses to figure out if their marketing strategies, based on analytics, are worth the effort.

Chapter 3

Real World Examples of Data Analytics Benefitting Businesses

Small Changes, Long Time Periods And Always Willing To Correct

Kroger supermarket chain is one of the most successful supermarket chains in the world. Aside from strong sales, an efficient work force and an excellent record for customer satisfaction, their true prowess comes in the form of how they use data analytics to improve themselves, consistently and intelligently. Kroger is a strong store because it is a strong brand. Kroger customers consistently rate their shopping experience and value at the store as 'excellent'. Kroger's success is the product of dedication to analytics, and using this information to make small changes over the years that have led to such strong brand loyalty. Analytics contextualizes large data sets and how they relate to a business, and Kroger had to make smart little changes to improve the numbers they were reading. One of the goals of Kroger was to increase the use of customer coupons in store. The reasoning here is that if customers are using coupons that were mailed to their homes, they would be driving customers to shop at Kroger. Nationwide statistics show that the rate in which customers use grocery coupons is about four percent, meaning 96% of all coupons end up in the trash or are never used. This is a huge waste of mail, printing, adjusting sale prices and creating coupon entries in computer systems. Think about this, for every coupon that is created, that barcode must be entered into a computer terminal and used throughout every store in the district where the coupon was mailed out. The costs are enormous, and the returns on coupons are quite poor. Supermarkets continue to mail coupons because even with a four percent return rate, the benefits are still worthwhile, whether in the form of coupons used or just advertising through the mail. Kroger, by comparison, has a coupon return rate of seventy percent, 66% above the national average. Kroger's coupon return rate was not always this high, and is the product of small changes done over a number of years.

Through hypothesis, experimentation and analytics on the results, Kroger has been able to create the greatest rate of returned coupons in the country. The tweaks they have made to the coupons they mail- range from color scheme, various price points, emphasizing discount percentage, trying different products and personalizing customer coupons. Their success today is a result of experiments conducted in each and every one of these categories over a number of decades. This is the key point I want to make with Kroger; they ran each experiment for a long enough period of time to effectively see if their changes were positively or negatively impacting revenue. The analytics were used to verify where their increased revenue was coming from, or for changes that were negative, to verify that changes had a negative impact. Kroger stuck with a decision for a minimum of one financial quarter before analyzing an idea to see if it was truly worthwhile. They stuck with bad ideas for a period of three months because a small time period would not provide an accurate picture of their revenue and the experiment's effectiveness. Your business will also be using hypothesis testing to increase sales and customer satisfaction; the lesson to take away is, Kroger managed successful changes through dedication to experimentation, only making small changes and then verifying the outcomes using analytics.

Micro Sales And Whales

Go onto the Apple app store or Google play store and you will notice that nearly all apps, particularly games, are free. It might seem counterintuitive, but free games make much more money than paid games. The revenue that game companies see on their products comes in two forms, advertising and small sales called 'micro-transactions.' Revenue from ads is a good chunk of their overall portfolio, but the real money comes from these very small transactions. What might be surprising to hear is that only 2.2% of users ever pay anything for these apps.

The process of creating this free-to-play model that most game companies follow was the processes of years of experimentation. Analytics were conducted consistently on products to see where revenue was coming from, as it wasn't always the opinion that free games were the most profitable. Analytics determined the tolerance consumers have for in-app purchases, with many games falling to the wayside because their small changes proved to be a worse business model. The 2.2% of people that do make in-app purchases spend enough money that 97.8% of the player base can enjoy the games for free. The small portion of consumers that do pay are referred to as 'whales', and just a few whales are necessary for thousands to enjoy a product for free.

This model is quite incredible and is the result of thousands of experiments involving different models of sales, and what items can be purchased. The overall result today might prove a sea of similarly themed games for consumers with similar purchases that can be made across all games, but the results enable the large player base that many of these games see.

The lesson here is that what might seem counterintuitive could prove to be the best model. Testing different models is the only reason that we have the prominent business model that we have today. For a small business, this is much more difficult to do, as you can only make so many changes and cannot risk trying counterintuitive approaches just to see the effect, but the lesson is still important. Experimentation can prove models that humans would never naturally come up with.

Matthew Adams

Chapter 4

A Step-By-Step Guide For Conducting Data Analysis For Your Business

Organizing Your Existing Data

The first step to utilizing data is to organize and categorize the data that you have. This necessary step is used so that software can analyze the data to find trends and correlations as well as solve various optimization problems. The categorization of data is also necessary for determining the additional data that your business may need to collect. Where this data has been previously stored will be vastly different depending on the business and the number of electric records that it keeps. Some basic records that all businesses have are employee salaries, employee health care costs, overhead costs broken down by category (electric, rent, etc.), total sales broken down into the smallest time scale that can easily be done, products sold with profit margins on each product, transactions done by cash and credit card and a few others that will be specific to your business.

The organization of data, and the accurate reporting of it, is extremely important for producing accurate results for every analytical statistic that you will look at. As you organize your data and create categories, mark the data that comes from electronic records. This will signify data that is absolutely accurate. In chapter two, we refereed to this data as *digital analytics.* To record this data, either use Microsoft Excel or a similar program.

For free software, Google Sheets offers a great software package that can save results in multiple formats.

Take your time with this first step, as I understand the arduous and repetitive nature of data entry for your small businesses. Believe me when I say that it becomes much easier when you have some existing data sets to work with. We want to have a decent number of categories for our data, because while you may know some of the problems you wish to solve, other problems in the future will use this data; you just don't know it yet.

Most of the data you enter will be recorded by the month, such as your utility bills and rent, as well as healthcare costs. The time measurement for salary is determined if your employees are paid by the hour, or on a yearly salary. You will want to input this data as one *unit*, meaning the dollar figure per time unit you decided with your employee. In the United States, 99% of the time, this is either hourly or yearly. The most important small unit time increment is in revenue generated; however, based on the firm, there are some exceptions. For most businesses, you will want revenue per hour; this is especially true with firms that operate with a customer facing store front. You will want the smallest time unit because many optimization problems are often solved on a per-hour unit of measurement, and revenue per hour can always be extrapolated to larger time scales. If your firm seeks revenue through contracted projects, or client accounts, recording your revenue is done slightly different.

In cases of contracted projects, you will want to list your revenue per hour, as well as how many hours each contract took to complete. For client accounts, you will want to make each client its own category, and here, list the revenue obtained on a time scale that makes sense for the particular business. For example, a financial planner would list this per year or small loan businesses would organize this per interest period. How we break down revenue and the categories it falls under is going to set how we visualize that data, or how we apply statistical models on those data sets.

Lastly, for any business operating by selling products directly to customers, the profit margin per product will be extremely useful for you. I understand that calculating this is not always easy, especially depending on the vendor, but it's worth taking the time to enter this data. If you sell many products and the calculation is arduous, select your five or ten most popular products and enter your profit margins for at least those products. You probably already have a profit margin in mind; however, you will want to include shipping, store and stocking in the margin. If you run a mechanic shop, the number of parts that you sell, especially with ordered parts, will be too large to do this effectively and you will only be selecting your most popular products. Your data will be organized somewhat different, as each product or service will need to include hours of labor and the profit margins for common parts.

Tools For Data Visualization

There are many different tools for visualizing your data, ranging in cost and purpose. This is a list of some of the most popular software tools and their common feature sets. For more information about visualizing data, as well as a statistic that should be used by more businesses, please refer to chapter five.

SAS – Software & Solutions, this company offers a diverse range of tools for visualizing your existing data, ultimately helping you to better understand the main profit drivers in your business. Their service includes optimization tools that are mainly built towards businesses selling individual products, and not contractual work. This is one of the most costly toolsets on this list, but their services are very in-depth. The cost of SAS might be worth it for their customer service; however, their forums are useful even if you do not use their software. Their customer base is large and the type of businesses they attract is diverse. You will find useful information on their forums because the questions asked can be applied to nearly all statistical software. I have seen some of their products in action, but personally, do not use them, as my own business is contractual, with a limited set of products sold. My brother used their software when operating a small chemical company, one that had hundreds of products to list with prices changing regularly from vendors. I've looked at some of their work, and certainly, if you offer many products it is worth a look. For my brother, the advantage came in organizing the cost of materials to determine costs for producing a custom made product. You can find their product page here:

http://www.sas.com/en_us/software/enterprise-solutions.html

Fusion Charts – For pure visualization of data, 'Fusion Charts' is probably your best bet on this list. The software itself is easy to use, and you can visualize your data before you pay for the full product. The trial software allows you to enter your data and use a handful of charts and graphs in a limited capacity. If you are a contractor and want to sort through the data you've accumulated, this is a good bet. For a small business, especially one that sells a number of products, 'Fusion Charts' is harder to recommend. There is one exception though; the tools are really great for presenting data to investors. You probably already know if you need outside money to expand your business, or if this is something that you are interested in pursuing. For statistical analysis and optimization problems, 'Fusion Charts' is extremely limited. Think about it as simply a tool for organizing data, presenting it visually and all at a pretty reasonable cost. One potential draw is the underpinning engine is based in Java, an extremely well known programming language. Hiring a third party to expand on what is included in the suite is certainly an option, but I'd really recommend using a dedicated product like SAS if you want to work on optimization. Their product page can be found here:

http://www.fusioncharts.com/tour

Google Charts – Free software for visualizing your data, I like to think about this as Fusion Charts lite. It will get the job done, but it won't be as pretty. There are a few advantages here that none of the other software packages have, mostly coming from the ever expanding nature of Google's API. While Google is well known for dropping support of several of its products, 'Google Charts' has been going strong for a number of years. If you are running a niche business and want a third party to help with running your data, Google Charts can easily be used to this effect. It's built in Java, just like Fusion Charts, but the code is neater. If you're not a computer programmer, this will mean little to you, but just know that if you are seeking outside help, 'Google Charts' is a good way of handing your data over to a third party. Google Charts can be found here:

https://developers.google.com/chart

Clear Story Data – If cost is not an issue, Clear Story is probably going to fit your needs. The advantage of their software package is the pool of data that is already stored within their suite. They have data from many different businesses, recorded anonymously, or through existing government data. This data can be used to solve optimization problems even if you yourself don't have every necessary piece of information. For example, a pharmacy could use their built in data to know expected orders based on national trends. By selecting your business type, Clear Story will help fill in additional information based on the data sets it has collected from similar businesses. This can be helpful if you have limited data sets, or if your data sets only cover a limited time period. The software does not have a clear price for the year and is negotiated on a per business basis. A thirty day trial can be purchased for $599, but a two week trail is free. Again, it's not cheap, but it comes with data that none of these other utilities can offer. Their tools are just as strong as SAS, and their data visualization is second to none. Their website can be found here:

http://www.clearstorydata.com/

Businesses Specific Analytics And Managing Tools – For your business sector, there are specific tools that you can purchase to aid you in a variety of different ways beyond visualization, projections and optimizations. The software available covers common businesses such as grocery stores, pharmacies and gas stations, as well as landlords and more. Each industry will have a few different packages available, and depending on what you want to accomplish, this could be your best bet. For example, Rent Manager Online is one of several competing tools used for landlords that have thirty or more units (you can use it if you have fewer, but the cost makes it less of a good option). No one feature is going to be better than SAS or Clear Story, and their visualization tools generally won't be any better than Google Charts, but what you do get are very niche specific features like ordering supplies automatically, or the best suited tools to keep track of scanned documents.

Social Media Analytics

It's likely that your business has some form of social media presence, whether through Twitter or Facebook. You may try and promote sales on these sites, use them for customer feedback, or simply have a page to cross off that box on a checklist. All of these are totally valid reasons for creating your social media page. Truly, how you use social media doesn't matter as much right now as how you can use social media to get a demonstration of simple analytics for your business. Using Google Analytics, you can get a sense of just some of the useful metrics that analytics can provide. Google Analytics is free to use (a small business should not pay for Google Analytics Premium) and offers a variety of measuring tools and stored data. A lot of this data will not increase your sales, and it might be hard to run optimizations on what Google provides, but I suggest you tinker on Google's webpage and take a look at peak traffic times to your social media page, how many unique users you get and peak times on larger scales like seasons or years. You can gleam some useful information such as growth in your online presence, or the number of attempts by hackers to take over your page, something every webpage must deal with.

If your business is online focused, Google Analytics will serve an entirely different role; it will be a fantastic source for gathering additional data. The information that Google has collected can easily be transferred into your existing data sets. You may want to use this information to test online advertisements to see what the magnitude of their effect is. You may simply want to see how users respond, in terms of activity, to posts you make on your web page. This is one of Google Analytics' strongest points, a great way for hypothesis testing. Discussed in chapter two, enterprise decision management is the incorporation of advanced data tools and hypothesis testing, so businesses can make the most informed decisions possible. You will have to keep track of how you are using your social media page for testing, but all of the data will automatically be stored by Google, and can be retrieved for free.

How To Conduct Data Analysis To Enhance Your Businesses

At this point, you should have already organized several data sets based on information already collected at your business. The next step is to decide on whether you want to solve a complex optimization problem such as the optimal opening and closing times of your business, or a simpler visual analyzation of where your revenue is coming from. Depending on what you wish to accomplish, you will use one of the appropriate software packages described earlier in this section. Visualization tools will provide you with new insight into your operating costs and where your revenue comes from, while optimization tools will provide *theoretical* answers to the problems you pose. This brings us to a very important part of business analytics. At the end of the day, analytics in business *is* hypothesis testing. This means that for whatever decision you make, whether it is where a product is placed on a shelf or the hours of your store, you must compare it to a second data set where that variable is different. Changing your store hours is a serious change, as you don't want to confuse your existing customer base; however, you will need to compare your revenue and operating costs to when your store hours were different. You cannot take it at faith value that any software package will always provide the best result. Optimizations in business will always require testing. For use of visualization tools, these are also best used for hypothesis testing. A common outcome of using visualization tools is attempting to promote items that have a higher profit margin, typically by up selling to a consumer or placing those products where customers are more likely to see them. The visualization tools have to be returned to after some time has passed to verify that the changes to your business have indeed increased revenue. Optimization is a process of small tweaks that lead to the best outcomes. We have already covered several examples of small businesses of all sorts benefitting from data analytics to solve optimization problems and increase customer happiness, both in this chapter and throughout most topics in this book.

In more general terms, there are things that every single business can do to increase their profits. Regardless of your business sector, I suggest looking at the total number of credit card payments you receive versus cash payments. Many small businesses implement credit card minimums, meaning a customer must use cash unless the purchase total exceeds a minimum value. This is almost always a mistake on the part of the small business, and the percentage of revenue lost to the major credit card companies is never as much as what you would gain if you accepted credit cards for purchases of any amount, or a significantly reduced minimum. To determine if your business is potentially losing out on revenue because of a minimum purchase, you must run a hypothesis test. Allow your business to accept credit payments on purchases of any amount for one to two months; you can then compare this to the average revenue that you saw in those same months for the last few years. Note that you will want to compare revenues to the same months of the year, and you cannot compare it to any one year, but rather an average of those months for all of the years you have data for; this will create the most accurate result.

Sustainable Success Through Data

Your willingness to test new business ideas and compare them how you previously operated your firm is the key to your success. The changes you make to your business are most useful when you gain data to back up or refute their usefulness. Make sure that as you adapt your business and solve for optimization problems, or if you are trying new products and services, that you are comparing the changes you have made to a proper time scale. Changes that you make that might negatively affect your bottom line should be followed through with enough time to verify that the effects are negative. In chapter three, Kroger supermarkets were taken as an example of hypothesis testing and analytics done right. There were entire financial quarters where they suffered because of experimentation, but it needed to be done to verify the results. When you make changes to your business, you must account for both the possible positive or negative effects. Do not attempt to make changes to your business or how it operates unless you are willing to endure potential negative effects; it is businesses that understand this, that use hypothesis testing and analytics to their strongest effect.

Risk Management Tips

Optimizing one's business and increasing revenue comes with inherent risk. You may alienate customers as your business changes to take on new challenges. You may have information problems with your customers as hours, staff or prices change in your business. This is the major risk of business optimization, and firms of all sizes must come to deal with this major issue. There are a couple of ways to mitigate the risk of losing customers as you adapt your business for increased profits; you must have clear messaging to your existing customer base and you must focus on small optimizations and not full on business overhauls.

Messaging the changes to your business to your existing clients can be done in a variety of ways, and depending on your business and its clientele, this could be best done in person, through social media or through flyers. Messaging is important because it amps up the process of seeing the changes in your business as you make optimizations. If you promote a new product that has increased profit margins, how long should you wait to verify that your placement changes were the right decision? This is a function of the foot traffic present in your business, but can be sped up through focused messaging. Even if a new product is placed front and center, you may want to advertise it in other sections of the store. This can be applied to contractual firms as well. A new service or promoting an existing one should be a priority when you are in the testing phase of optimization. It is during these experimental periods where social media can be a great asset. Depending on your reach online, you can signal new products and services clearly, but do not discount the useful feedback you can receive as well. There is a risk in asking for customer feedback in a public forum; however the information gained is often worth this risk. Getting a feel for how customers like store changes can encourage your smart changes; if feedback is overly negative, it can save you the agony of sticking to a change that is not helpful to your business.

Hypothesis testing comes up time and time again in business optimization, but what is often lost is just how close this is to scientific experimentation. The crux of hypothesis testing is *small* changes as to test only what is being changed and nothing else. Remember that you are trying to improve your business, not conduct a full overhaul of your services and products. You should not need to do a full revamp of what your firm does and how it serves its customers. Focus on just a few optimizations at a time. By doing this, you mitigate the risk of adverse customer effects by reducing the impact negative changes can make to your bottom line. Also, you localize each business change that your are testing.

Offering a full suite of new products does not help you in understanding how any one product can benefit your store. The data from multiple product changes will distort the effects seen on the product that you were originally trying to promote.

Chapter 5

Variance And Covariance In Business

Statistics and visual representations of data is a necessity for the true comprehension of what the data means as a whole. Data is too numerous and complex to be analyzed by the individual datum, and various visualizations of data aid in understanding the complexity and use cases for any one set of data, or multiple sets of data as compared to each other. In chapter four, you read about the importance of several software packages that can visualize data for easier interpretation. The metrics used to make those charts are equally important and are based on the statistical analysis.

Depending on your business, its size and the products and services provided, basic statistical information will have more or less significance. In chapter one, we discussed the use of averages, modes and regressions, as well as a brief discussion of magnitudes. All of these metrics are important when looking at the messages hidden with large swaths of data, but I want to impart with you two more basic statistical calculations that are useful.

Other useful statistics come in the form of variance and covariance, which will be useful to most firms. Statistical software will sometimes label these differently depending on the knowledge base that they expect from the user; however, their utility will always remain the same. Variance is the difference between the average of a data set and any given number within that set. This number can be used to determine how closely related datum are within a set. In practical terms, if all items in a store are categorized and the variance is computed on their prices, this will tell us how far off any given product is in price from the average of the store. This can be useful in cases of looking to eliminate products that are priced outside of what your customers are willing to pay. A price above the variance would be a good measure of where this line could be drawn. Covariance is the relationship between any two given numbers and how they change with each other. This is useful on data showing the demand for a number of products. Business owners can determine, based on the covariance, which items are taking the same place in the minds of consumers, knowing where exists product or service overlap and possibly reducing the prominence of one product to bolster the other. Both of these statistical methods can be displayed in a variety of ways, ranging from bar graphs of variance for each product or service, to quarterly plots of whole sections of products and how they negatively or positively affect other sections of a store.

Chapter 6

Effective Data Management

The most useful analytics come from data that is stored properly, categorized correctly and mined thoroughly. To effectively store and use the data your business collects, you must first incorporate these four steps:

Data Management – The way in which data is organized to be processed by a computer; data management has changed significantly over the last half century. Today, data can be stored non-sequentially and still used effectively. The usefulness of proper data management has not been lost, as its principles extend far beyond how data is stored. Data must be verified before it can be used, and there needs to be a built-in timeline for the life of this data. Data gained from surveys and customer data needs to be checked to look for outliers and incorrect entries. Data eventually becomes irrelevant as consumer demands, demographics and offered products change. Expect that data gained from your business will have a finite lifespan. In terms of storage and categorization, in chapter four, we discussed the best practices for finding useful data in your business. How you store this data and its usefulness comes down to how you categorize data and the time scale that you measure it. For wages and revenue, we try and work in small time scales, whereas for overhead costs, we work in month-long time scales.

Data Mining – Depending on the scale of your business and what your data management needs are, data mining will range in forms of complexity. With data mining, we gain insight into large data sets by running a series of examinations on data to try and make sense of emerging patterns, or lack thereof. In its simplest form, this can be running a regression analysis on two large data sets, and searching for a correlation. Data mining is commonly confused as looking for useful data in information that is already stored; however, what is really being mined, are patterns and the significance of large data sets. You can think of this as the exploratory analysis that was discussed in chapter one.

Data Integration – Combining data sets so that they can be analyzed as a whole is referred to as data integration. In business terms, it is most commonly used during company mergers and acquisitions. In these situations, large troves of data exist from two companies that provide similar services and products. To get the most out of all of this data, the data needs to be combined, removing data that is not relevant to both sets. For businesses outside of merges, data integration can also come in the form of using data from similar firms. Some of the software packages described in chapter four, such as Clear Story Data, will integrate data from other businesses and public records.

Data Warehousing – Using data from sources that do not have any immediate relation, we refer to records of analysis and integration of this disparate data as data warehousing. For businesses of a small size, this can come in the form of using public records to bolster analysis in a particular topic. For larger businesses, this comes in using data from large firms that specialize in different disciplines. While the relationship between the data is not directly correlated, similarities in the size of the firm or how the data can be used makes this a necessary step in data synthesis.

Working Together

Data management, data mining, data integration and data warehousing work together to form the types of analysis that benefit businesses the most. Each component is necessary for different forms of analysis. Starting with data management, the verification and categorization of data sets makes the data workable to a business. Data mining is a repeated step and is the scanning of data for useful patterns and statistics. This is done through regressions among data sets and other statistical data to find emerging patterns that describe the data as a whole. Data integration is the combining of data sets across multiple businesses, bolstering the data that can be mined from any one source of data. Data warehousing is the merging of data sets that are not related to each other for types of analysis that cannot be done on any one data set. For data warehousing, imagine a company using its own records for sales of a product or service, and correlating this with data from public records on public transportation pickup locations. The two data sets have nothing in common, but can be combined if the goal is to relate sales of a product to a demographic that uses this form of transportation. These data sets together fall into the category of data management, and can then be used for further mining or data integration.

How To Handle And Manage Big Data

Regardless of the size of your business, there are several principles necessary to get the most out of your data. A key challenge, depending on the size of your firm, is the exponential increase in data that is collected and processed. Handling such large quantities of data and processing it efficiently can be a challenge, but following these rules will aid you in this process: You must store data in a central location that can be accessed and processed through multiple sources. Data must be sifted through to remove common duplicates, particularly after data integration. Data must be protected and secured, wiping customer footprints off personal data when possible. Depending on the amount of data, it may be best to use a third party such as Amazon, or backup data yourself to prevent the loss of information. Sensitive data must be disposed of at regular intervals and customers made aware of data retention.

Depending on your business, each and every one of these principles will range in necessity and feasibility. It's most important that data be kept in a state where it can be processed by multiple programs, and the best way to do this is the proper categorization of data, as well as a standardization of data retrieval. Disposing of customer data after a given time is a step for all businesses, but equally as strong is wiping the customer footprint from said data. This means turning data with identifiable information into metadata that can be used, but not tracked back to individuals.

The security of your data also depends greatly on the size of your firm. A very small business can store data locally, and even backup this data themselves. The cost of storage is cheap enough that this is a reasonable solution for many businesses. When going this route, access to where this data is stored must be handled responsibly. Granting access to this data to multiple users across a network will likely be a necessity, but ensuring the data repository is kept on a secure computer is dire. Cloud services solve data storage and access for a great many of larger firms, and backing up this data locally is an option, as well as paying additional fees for duplicates in case a cloud server malfunctions. This will depend on the company from whom you purchase cloud services. Amazon insures data with backups up to a certain size, but additional backups can be created for a fee. Microsoft, as well as several other companies, has a competing service. The best option for your business will be a function of data quantity, security needs and how many users need regular access to data.

Chapter 7

Hubris And The Limitations Of Big Data

Unintended Consequences Of Automation

CVS pharmacy ran an experiment a few years ago to reduce the instances of theft across its stores. It took the items that were frequently stolen and automatically encased them in a more secure packaging, packaging that could only be removed by an employee. Items that received this treatment were razor blades and batteries, common items that would be shoplifted. An unintended consequence of this experiment was the accidental discrimination of a large portion of its customer base.

The 'Just For Men products' sold via CVS was the next set of items to be encased in the more secure packaging. There was an incredible oversight; however, not *every* product was given the new security improvement. The algorithm that determined which products needed the beefed up security did not account for accidental racism, and when 'Just For Men products' that were more commonly used by African Americans became more secure, there was a reasonable outcry of discrimination on the part of CVS. The automation through analytics here is a key reason why human intervention is needed at key points in the decision-making process. While Amazon's recommended products page is harmless, CVS's attempt to secure its product was a public relations disaster. If management was involved in the decision process, it's quite possible the 'Just For Men dye' would have still been secured, but the encasing would have been given to the entire line of products, not just those that target a particular demographic.

The Human Element – Proper Analytics With Improper Analysis

Public school districts across the United States have a strong focus on state and federal testing. They are incentivized to care a great deal about these tests, as it determines the funding that each school receives. The growing need to improve test scores among students has led to the widespread use of analytics throughout public schools. This analysis is done well before the date of the test, and basic statistical information is given to teachers so that they can get a better sense of how their students are doing. There is a lesson being taught throughout American classrooms, but students are not on the receiving end. The lesson is 'statistics that are analyzed poorly have no effect at best, and can have adverse effects at worst'.

Teachers are given the average test scores of their classrooms, as well as a handful of other statistical data. Using this assortment of data points, they are supposed to improve the test scores of their students. How the data is measured and when the data is measured is removed from the teacher. They know that it comes from previous test data, but with the limited information, the data provides little actionable information. Instead, what many teachers adopted was a goal of raising the class average by seeking out students that could gain the most improvement. This will raise the class average, and a small portion of students increased their test scores. What this fails to do is take into account the large portion of students for whom the test scores stayed the same, the students that were already at the bottom. The poor statistical data presented to teachers could only be used in a way that would negatively affect the class as a whole. Focusing on metrics that the district has said are important; teachers are unable to teach to the entire classroom.

There is a lesson in how some American teachers are treating data on their students. While they are using it to raise the metrics provided, the metrics themselves do not give an accurate picture of the entire classroom. Worse, the statistics measured by the school are not the same as the statistics used to determine funding. Individual students are the key factor in determining funding, and a teacher's focus on a limited set of those students to raise the artificial metrics set by school districts, has resulted in increased setback in an already struggling area of the country's education system.

Conclusion

Thank you again for purchasing *Data Analytics: Using Big Data Analytics For Business To Increase Profits And Create Happy Customers.*

I hope this book was able to inform you on how data can improve your business. This book has gone over a variety of ways in which data can be recorded, stored and utilized by firms of various sizes. Whether your business is service-oriented or product driven, analytics can improve your revenue and better satisfy your customers.

The next step is to organize and categorize the data you already have. From there, you will want to graph this data and produce the simple statistics that will help you describe this information. I hope that you decide to work on several different optimization problems in your firm, using hypothesis testing and further data collection to improve your business. You have the information that you need to manage data and the software recommendations to process this data. It's time to get to work and improve your business using informed, statistics-driven information.

Finally, if you enjoyed this book, please be sure to leave a review on Amazon. It'd be greatly appreciated!

Thank you and good luck.

CPSIA information can be obtained
at www.ICGtesting.com
Printed in the USA
LVHW081847140822
725923LV00008B/711

9 781540 380036